Beginner's Path in C#: A Simplified Approach

AF893755

Learning C# with Real-World Examples and Applications

Alex Coder

Beginner's Path in C#: A Simplified Approach

This document is geared towards providing exact and reliable information with regards to the topic and issue covered. The publication is sold with the idea that the publisher is not required to render accounting, officially permitted, or otherwise, qualified services. If advice is necessary, legal or professional, a practiced individual in the profession should be ordered.

From a Declaration of Principles which was accepted and approved equally by a Committee of the American Bar Association and a Committee of Publishers and Associations.

The information herein is offered for informational purposes solely, and is universal as so. The presentation of the information is without contract or any type of guarantee assurance.

The trademarks that are used are without any consent, and the publication of the trademark is without permission or backing by the trademark owner. All trademarks and brands within this book are for clarifying purposes only and are owned by the owners themselves, not affiliated with this document.

TABLE OF CONTENTS

Chapter 1: Embark on Your C# Journey

Embark on Your C# Journey

Setting the Stage

Imagine a world where everyday objects come alive with interactive capabilities, where software applications seamlessly blend into our daily routines. This captivating realm is made possible through the power of programming languages like C#. As you embark on this journey, you're about to unlock a universe of possibilities, where your ideas can take tangible form and your creativity knows no bounds. **The Unsung Heroes: Developers**

Before we delve into the intricacies of C#, let's take a moment to appreciate the unsung heroes who make our digital experiences possible: developers. These individuals possess a unique blend of creativity, problem-solving skills, and unwavering determination. They are the architects of the software that powers our smartphones, computers, and innumerable other devices that have become indispensable in our modern lives.

Why C#?

In the vast landscape of programming languages, C# stands out as a versatile and powerful choice. Developed by Microsoft, this object-oriented language has gained widespread popularity due to its flexibility, scalability, and ease of use. Whether you're interested in building desktop applications, mobile apps, games, or even exploring the realms of artificial intelligence and machine learning, C# provides a solid foundation to bring your ideas to life.

The Fundamentals

Like any journey, learning C# begins with mastering the fundamentals. Let's break it down into bite-sized pieces:

Data Types and Variables

Data types are the building blocks of any program. They define the type of information you can store and manipulate. C# offers a variety of data types, including integers, floating-point numbers, booleans, and strings. Variables act as containers for these data types, allowing you to store and retrieve information as needed.

Control Structures

Control structures are the decision-makers in your code. They determine the flow of execution based on certain conditions or loops. Think of them as the traffic signals that guide your program through various paths, ensuring it performs the desired actions.

Functions and Methods

Functions and methods are reusable blocks of code that perform specific tasks. They allow you to break down complex problems into smaller, more manageable pieces. By encapsulating related functionality into functions or methods, you can create modular and maintainable code.

Object-Oriented Programming (OOP)

One of the core principles of C# is objectoriented programming (OOP). OOP is a programming paradigm that revolves around the concept of objects, which are instances of classes. These classes encapsulate data (properties) and behavior (methods), making it easier to organize and manage complex software systems.

- **Classes and Objects**: Classes are blueprints that define the characteristics and behavior of objects. Objects are instances of these classes, each with its own unique set of data and methods.

- **Inheritance**: Inheritance allows you to create new classes based on existing ones, inheriting their properties and methods. This promotes code reuse and facilitates the creation of hierarchical relationships between classes.
- **Encapsulation**: Encapsulation is the practice of bundling data and methods into a single unit (class), ensuring data integrity and controlling access to the class members.
- **Polymorphism**: Polymorphism enables objects of different classes to be treated as instances of a common base class. This allows for flexibility and extensibility in your code.

Real-World Applications

Now that you have a solid foundation in C#, let's explore some real-world applications where this language shines:

- **Windows Applications**: C# is widely used for building desktop applications for the Windows operating system, leveraging the powerful .NET Framework or .NET Core.
- **Web Development**: With the introduction of ASP.NET, C# has become a popular choice for developing dynamic and interactive web applications.
- **Game Development**: C# is a preferred language for game development, especially in the Unity game engine, which has a thriving community of developers.
- **Mobile Development**: With the advent of Xamarin, developers can use C# to create cross-platform mobile applications for iOS, Android, and Windows devices.

Embracing the Community

One of the greatest strengths of C# lies in its vibrant and supportive community. From online forums and discussion boards to local meetups and conferences, you'll find a wealth of resources and opportunities to learn, share, and collaborate with fellow developers.

Immerse yourself in this community, ask questions, contribute to open-source projects, and stay up-to-date with the latest trends and best practices. The journey of learning never ends, and the C# community is here to support you every step of the way.

Conclusion

As you embark on your C# journey, remember that learning a programming language is an ongoing process of discovery and growth. Embrace the challenges, celebrate your successes, and never stop exploring the vast possibilities that C# offers. With dedication, perseverance, and a touch of creativity, you'll soon find yourself crafting innovative solutions and leaving your mark on the digital landscape.

So, take that first step, fire up your code editor, and let your imagination soar. The world of C# awaits, and the only limit is the boundaries of your own creativity. Happy coding!

Introduction to C# and .NET

C# (pronounced "C-sharp") is a modern, general-purpose, object-oriented programming language developed by Microsoft. It was created in 2000 and has become one of the most popular programming languages, particularly for building Windows desktop applications and games.

Some key features of C#:

1. **Object-Oriented**: C# is a true objectoriented language that supports concepts like encapsulation, inheritance, and polymorphism.

2. **Type-safe**: C# is a type-safe language, meaning that it performs type checking at compile-time to catch type-related errors early in the development process.

3. **Managed Code**: C# is a managed code language, meaning that it relies on the .NET Common Language Runtime (CLR) to handle memory management and other low-level tasks, making it easier to write secure and robust code.

4. **Modern Syntax**: C# has a clean, modern syntax that is easy to read and write, making it a great choice for beginners and experienced developers alike.

5. **Versatile**: C# can be used for a wide range of applications, including desktop applications, web applications, mobile apps, games, and more.

.NET Framework and .NET Core

C# is tightly integrated with the .NET

Framework and .NET Core, which are software frameworks developed by Microsoft.

The **.NET Framework** is a software framework that runs primarily on Windows. It provides a runtime environment (the Common Language Runtime or CLR) and a vast class library that simplifies the development of Windows desktop applications, web applications, and web services.

.NET Core is a modern, open-source, and cross-platform implementation of .NET. It was designed to be modular and lightweight, making it suitable for a wide range of applications, including cloud-based services, IoT, and mobile apps. .NET Core can run on Windows, macOS, and Linux.

Both the .NET Framework and .NET Core provide a rich set of libraries and tools for building applications, handling tasks like networking, file access, database connectivity, and more.

Development Tools

Microsoft provides several development tools for working with C# and .NET, including:

1. **Visual Studio**: A powerful Integrated Development Environment (IDE) for Windows that supports C#, Visual Basic, F#, and other languages. Visual Studio provides a rich set of tools for coding, debugging, testing, and deploying applications.

2. **Visual Studio Code**: A lightweight, cross-platform code editor that supports C# and other languages through extensions.

3. **.NET CLI**: A cross-platform commandline interface (CLI) for building and running .NET Core applications.

Whether you're a beginner or an experienced developer, C# and .NET offer a robust and versatile platform for building a wide range of applications. With its modern syntax, powerful tools, and extensive class libraries, C# and .NET can help you develop high-quality software more efficiently.

Setting Up Your Development Environment

1. **Install Visual Studio**: Microsoft Visual Studio is the most popular Integrated Development Environment (IDE) for C# and .NET development. You can download the latest version of Visual Studio from the official Microsoft website (https://visualstudio.microsoft.com/downloads/). During the installation process, make sure to select the ".NET desktop development" workload, which includes the necessary

components for building desktop applications with C# and .NET.

2. **Install .NET Core SDK**: If you plan to develop cross-platform applications with .NET Core, you'll need to install the .NET Core SDK. You can download the latest version from the official

   .NET website (https://dotnet.microsoft.com/download). The .NET Core SDK includes the command-line interface (CLI) tools and the runtime required to build and run .NET Core applications.

3. **Create a New Project**: Once you have Visual Studio installed, you can create a new project. Open Visual Studio and go to "File" > "New" > "Project". In the "Create a new project" window, select the project type you want to create (e.g., Console App, Windows Forms App, ASP.NET Core Web App, etc.) and click "Next". Follow the prompts to configure your project settings,

such as the project name and location, and then click "Create".

4. **Understand the Project Structure**: After creating a new project, Visual Studio will generate a basic project structure for you. This structure typically includes folders for your source code files, project configuration files, and other resources. Take some time to familiarize yourself with the project structure and understand the purpose of each file and folder.

5. **Write Your First Code**: With your project created, you can now start writing code! Depending on the project type, Visual Studio will create a default entry point for your application (e.g., Program.cs for a Console App, Form1.cs for a Windows Forms App). You can start by modifying this file or creating new files as needed.

6. **Build and Run**: Once you've written some code, you can build and run your application. In Visual Studio, you can use the "Build" menu or the keyboard shortcut (typically Ctrl+Shift+B) to build your project. To run your application, you can use the "Debug" menu or the keyboard shortcut (typically F5).

7. **Debug and Test**: Visual Studio provides excellent debugging tools that allow you to step through your code, inspect variables, and identify and fix issues. You can set breakpoints, use the debugger windows (e.g., Watch, Locals, Call Stack), and utilize other debugging features to ensure your code is working as expected.

8. **Learn and Explore**: As you gain more experience with C# and .NET, you'll want to explore additional features and tools. Visual Studio offers a vast ecosystem of extensions, templates, and tools to enhance your development experience. Additionally,

there are many online resources, documentation, and communities dedicated to C# and .NET development that can help you continue learning and improving your skills.

Setting up your development environment is the first step in your journey with C# and .NET. Once you have everything set up correctly, you'll be ready to start building your applications and exploring the powerful features of this popular programming language and framework.

Your First C# Program

Let's dive into your first C# program! We'll start with a simple console application that will print a message to the console window.

1. **Open Visual Studio**: Launch Visual Studio on your computer.

2. **Create a New Project**: Click on "Create a new project" (or go to "File" > "New"

   > "Project"). In the "Create a new project" window, select "Console App (.NET Core)" from the list of project templates. Click "Next".

3. **Configure Your Project**: In the next window, give your project a name (e.g., "MyFirstCSharpApp") and choose a location to save it. Make sure the project framework is set to the latest version of .NET Core. Click "Create".

4. **Open the Program.cs File**: In the Solution Explorer (usually on the righthand side of the Visual Studio window), expand the project node and locate the Program.cs file. Double-click it to open it in the code editor.

5. **Write the Code**: In the Program.cs file, you'll see a class named Program with a Main method. This is the entry point of your console application. Replace

the existing code in the Main method with the following:

csharp Copy

```
static void Main(string[] args)
{
   Console.WriteLine("Hello, World!");
   Console.ReadLine();
}
```

Here's what's happening:

- Console.WriteLine("Hello, World!"); will print the message "Hello, World!" to the console window.
- Console.ReadLine(); will pause the program and wait for the user to press Enter before closing the console window. This is useful for console applications so you can see the output before the program exits.

6. **Build and Run**: Now that you've written your code, you can build and run your program. You can do this by clicking the "Start" button (green triangle) in the Visual Studio toolbar, or by pressing F5 on your keyboard.
7. **See the Output**: A new console window should open, displaying the message "Hello, World!". The program will pause after printing the message, waiting for you to press Enter before closing the console window.

Congratulations! You've just written and run your first C# program. This simple example demonstrates the basic structure of a C# console application and how to print output to the console.

You can build upon this foundation by exploring more C# syntax, language features, and the vast .NET class libraries. With practice and dedication, you'll soon be able to create more complex and sophisticated applications using C# and .NET.

Understanding the Structure of a C# Program

1. **Namespaces**:

- Namespaces are used to organize code into logical groups and prevent naming conflicts.
- In a C# program, you'll typically see one or more using statements at the top, which import the required namespaces.
- Example: using System;

1. **Class**:

- Classes are the fundamental building blocks of objectoriented programming in C#.
- A class defines the properties and methods that an object of that class will have.

- In a console application, you'll have a class that contains the Main method, which is the entry point of the program.

2. **Main Method**:

- The Main method is the starting point of execution for a C# program.
- It has a specific signature: static void Main(string[] args).
- static means the method can be called without creating an instance of the class.
- void means the method doesn't return a value.
- string[] args is an array of strings that can be used to pass command-line arguments to the program.

3. **Statements and Expressions**:

- Statements are the basic instructions that make up a program, such as variable declarations, assignments, method calls, and control flow statements (e.g., if, for, while).

- Expressions are combinations of values, variables, operators, and function calls that evaluate to a single value.

4. **Variables and Data Types**:

- Variables are used to store data values during the program's execution.
- C# has various built-in data types, such as int (integer), double (doubleprecision floating-point), bool (boolean), string (tex t), and more.
- You can also define your own custom data types using classes and structs.

5. **Methods**:

- Methods are blocks of code that perform specific tasks and can be called from other parts of the program.

- Methods can optionally take parameters and return a value.
- Methods help to modularize code and promote reusability.

6. **Control Flow**:

- Control flow statements, such as if, else, for, while, and switch, control the order in which statements are executed based on certain conditions.
- These statements allow you to create branching logic and loops in your program.

7. **Comments**:

- Comments are code annotations that are ignored by the compiler.
- They are used to document your code, explain its purpose, or temporarily disable parts of the code.
- Single-line comments start with //, and multi-line comments are enclosed between /* and */.

Here's an example that demonstrates some of these components:

csharp

Copy

```
// Using the System namespace using

System;


// Defining a class named Program class

Program

{

  // The Main method is the entry point of
the program

  static void Main(string[] args)

  {

    // Declaring a variable and assigning a
value

    int age = 25;
```

```
        // Calling a method and storing the
result
        string message = GetGreeting(age);

        // Printing the message to the console
        Console.WriteLine(message);
    }

    // A method that returns a greeting
based on age
    static string GetGreeting(int age)
    {
        if (age < 18)
            return "Hello, young one!";
else
            return "Hello, wise one!";
    }
```

```
}
```

By understanding these structural elements, you'll be better equipped to read, write, and maintain C# programs effectively.

Chapter 2: Mastering the Fundamentals

1. **Data Types and Variables**:

- Understand the different data types available in C# (integers, floating-point numbers, booleans, characters, strings, etc.).
- Learn how to declare and initialize variables of different data types.
- Explore type conversion and casting between data types.

- Understand the concepts of value types and reference types.

Operators and Expressions:

- Study the various operators available in C# (arithmetic, assignment, comparison, logical, bitwise, etc.).
- Learn how to construct and evaluate expressions using operators and operands.
- Understand operator precedence and associativity rules.

Control Flow Statements:

- Master the use of if, else, switch, and conditional operator (?:) for decision-making.
- Learn how to use for, while, dowhile, foreach, and other loops for iteration.
- Understand how to use break, continue, and goto statements for controlling loop flow.

3. Methods:

- Learn how to define and call methods in C#.

- Understand method signatures, return types, and parameters (including optional and named parameters).
- Explore method overloading and recursive methods.

4. **Arrays and Collections**:

- Study how to declare, initialize, and manipulate arrays (singledimensional and multidimensional).
- Explore the various collection types in C# (lists, dictionaries, sets, etc.) and their common operations.

5. **Object-Oriented Programming (OOP)**:

- Understand the core principles of OOP: encapsulation, inheritance, and polymorphism.

- Learn how to define and work with classes, objects, properties, methods, and constructors.
- Explore access modifiers (public, private, protected, inter nal) for controlling accessibility.
- Study inheritance and how to create derived classes from base classes.
- Understand abstract classes and interfaces for implementing polymorphism.

6. **Exception Handling**:

- Learn how to handle exceptions using try, catch, finally, and throw statements.
- Understand different types of exceptions and when to throw custom exceptions.

7. **File I/O and Serialization**:

- Study how to read from and write to files using streams and reader/writer classes.
- Explore serialization techniques for converting objects to and from different formats (XML, JSON, binary, etc.).

8. **Debugging and Unit Testing**:

- Learn how to use the Visual Studio debugger and other debugging tools effectively.
- Understand the importance of unit testing and how to write and run unit tests using frameworks like MSTest or NUnit.

9. **LINQ and Lambda Expressions**:

- Explore LINQ (Language Integrated Query) for querying and manipulating data from various sources (arrays, collections, databases, XML, etc.).

- Learn how to use lambda expressions for writing concise and readable code.

10. **Asynchronous Programming**:

- Understand the need for asynchronous programming and how it can improve application performance and responsiveness.
- Learn how to use async and await keywords for writing asynchronous code.

As you practice and apply these fundamentals, you'll gradually build a solid foundation in C#. Additionally, explore the extensive .NET class libraries, which provide a wealth of functionality for various tasks, such as working with strings, dates, files, databases, networking, and more.

Regular practice, reading documentation, and seeking help from online resources and communities will help you master the fundamentals and become a proficient C# developer.

Variables and Data Types

Variables:

A variable is a named location in memory that can store a value. Variables in C# must be declared with a specific data type before they can be used. The syntax for declaring a variable is: csharp Copy

dataType variableName; For

example:

csharp Copy

int age;

After declaring a variable, you can assign a value to it using the assignment operator =:

csharp

Copy age

= 25;

You can also declare and initialize a variable in a single step:

csharp Copy

int age = 25;

Data Types:
C# provides several built-in data types, which can be categorized as value types and reference types.

Value Types:
Value types store their values directly in memory. When you assign a value type to a new variable, a copy of the original value is created. Some common value types are:

- int (32-bit signed integer)
- long (64-bit signed integer)
- float (32-bit floating-point number)

- double (64-bit floating-point number)
- bool (boolean, either true or false)
- char (16-bit Unicode character)

Reference Types:
Reference types store a reference to the memory location where the actual data is stored. When you assign a reference type to a new variable, a copy of the reference is created, not the data itself. Some common reference types are:

- string (sequence of characters)
- Classes (user-defined types)
- Arrays
- Delegates
- Interfaces

Type Conversion:
C# allows you to convert between compatible data types using explicit or implicit conversions.

Implicit Conversion:
Implicit conversion happens automatically when the target data type can accommodate the source data type without loss of precision or data. For example:

csharp Copy

int x = 10;

long y = x; // Implicit conversion from int to long

Explicit Conversion:
Explicit conversion is required when the target data type cannot accommodate the source data type without potential loss of precision or data. You must explicitly cast the value using the target data type. For example: csharp

Copy double x =

3.14;

int y = (int)x; // Explicit conversion from double to int (y = 3)

Type Safety:
C# is a type-safe language, meaning that variables must be explicitly declared with a data type, and type conversions must follow strict rules to ensure data integrity and prevent unexpected behavior.

Understanding variables and data types is crucial for writing correct and efficient code in C#. Proper use of data types and type conversions can help you avoid bugs, optimize memory usage, and write more readable and maintainable code.

Operators and Expressions

Operators:
An operator is a symbol that performs a specific operation on one or more operands (values or variables). C# provides various types of operators, including:

1. **Arithmetic Operators**: Used for performing mathematical operations such as addition

(+), subtraction (-), multiplication (*), division (/), and modulus (%).

2. **Assignment Operators**: Used for assigning values to variables. The basic assignment operator is =, but C# also provides compound assignment operators like +=, -=, *=, and /=.

3. **Comparison Operators**: Used for comparing values. Examples include == (equal to), != (not equal to), > (greater than), < (less than), >= (greater than or equal to), and <= (less than or equal to).

4. **Logical Operators**: Used for combining or inverting boolean expressions. The logical operators are && (and), || (or), and ! (not).

5. **Bitwise Operators**: Used for performing operations on individual bits of integer values. Examples include & (bitwise AND), | (bitwise OR), ^ (bitwise XOR), ~ (bitwise complement), << (left shift), and >> (right shift).

6. **Increment and Decrement Operators**: Used for increasing or decreasing the value of a variable by 1. The operators are ++ (increment) and -- (decrement).

7. **Conditional Operators**: The ternary conditional operator ?: is used for making simple if-else decisions.

8. **Other Operators**: C# also provides operators for type casting ((), as, is), null checking (??), and more.

Expressions:
An expression is a combination of operands, operators, and function calls that evaluates to a single value. Expressions can be as simple as a single value or variable, or they can be complex combinations of operators and subexpressions.

Here are some examples of expressions in C#: csharp Copy

```
int x = 10;        // A simple value expression
int y = x + 5;     // An arithmetic expression (y = 15)
bool isEven = y % 2 == 0; // A comparison expression (isEven = true)

// Complex expression involving multiple operators and subexpressions
int z = (x * 2) + (int)Math.Pow(y, 2); // z = 20 + 225 = 245
```

Operator Precedence and Associativity: When multiple operators are used in an expression, operator precedence and associativity determine the order in which operations are performed.

- **Operator Precedence**: Certain operators have higher precedence than others. For example, multiplication and division have higher precedence than addition and subtraction.

- **Associativity**: When multiple operators of the same precedence are present, associativity determines the order of evaluation (left-to-right or right-to-left).

You can use parentheses () to override the default precedence and associativity rules and explicitly control the order of operations in an expression.

Understanding operators and expressions is crucial for manipulating data and performing calculations in your C# programs. By mastering these concepts, you can write more efficient and readable code, and avoid common pitfalls related to operator precedence and associativity.

Control Structures (If Statements, Loops)

If Statements:

The if statement is used to execute a block of code conditionally, based on a boolean expression. The basic syntax is:

csharp Copy

```
if (condition)
{
    // Code to execute if condition is true
}
```

You can also include an else clause to specify a block of code to execute when the condition is false:

csharp

Copy

```
if (condition)
{
    // Code to execute if condition is true
}
else
```

```
{
   // Code to execute if condition is false
}
```

Additionally, you can chain multiple conditions using else if statements:

csharp Copy

```
if (condition1)
{
   // Code to execute if condition1 is true
}
else if (condition2)
{
   // Code to execute if condition1 is false
and condition2 is true
}
else
{
```

// Code to execute if both condition1 and condition2 are false

}

The ternary operator (?:) can also be used for simple if-else scenarios:

csharp Copy

int max = (a > b) ? a : b;

Loops:
Loops are used to repeatedly execute a block of code as long as a certain condition is met. C# provides several types of loops:

1. **For Loop**:
   The for loop is used when you know the number of iterations in advance. Its syntax is:

csharp Copy

for (initialization; condition; iteration)

{

// Code to execute for each iteration

```
}
```

2. **While Loop**:

   The while loop is used when you don't know the number of iterations in advance, but you have a condition that determines when to stop. Its syntax is:

```
csharp Copy
while (condition)
{
    // Code to execute while condition is true
}
```

3. **Do-While Loop**:

   The do-while loop is similar to the while loop, but it executes the loop body at least once, even if the condition is initially false. Its syntax is:

csharp

Copy do

```
{
   // Code to execute
} while (condition);
```

4. **Foreach Loop**:
   The foreach loop is used to iterate over the elements in a collection (e.g., array, list, or other enumerable types).
   Its syntax is:

csharp Copy

```
foreach (type item in collection)
{
   // Code to execute for each item in the
collection
}
```

5. **Break and Continue**:

The break statement is used to exit a loop prematurely, while the continue statement skips the current iteration and moves to the next one.

Control structures are essential for writing efficient and robust programs. By using if statements and loops, you can create complex logic, make decisions based on conditions, and iterate over data structures. As you progress in your C# programming journey, you'll encounter more advanced control structures and scenarios where their proper use becomes increasingly important.

Methods and Method Overloading

Methods are reusable blocks of code that perform a specific task. They are fundamental to procedural programming and object-oriented programming (OOP) in

C#. In this lesson, we'll explore methods and method overloading.

Defining Methods:
In C#, a method is defined within a class or struct. Here's the basic syntax for defining a method: csharp Copy

```
access_modifier return_type
MethodName(parameters)

{

   // Method body

   // Code to execute

   return value; // If the method returns a
value

}
```

- access_modifier specifies the accessibility of the method, such as public, private, protected, or internal.
- return_type is the data type of the value returned by the method. If the method

doesn't return a value, use the void keyword.

- MethodName is the name you give to the method, following standard naming conventions.
- parameters is an optional commaseparated list of parameters that the method can accept. Each parameter has a data type and a name.

Here's an example of a simple method that adds two integers:

csharp Copy

```
public int AddNumbers(int a, int b)
{
   int sum = a + b;
return sum;
}
```

Calling Methods:

To use a method, you need to call it from another part of your code. Method calls can be made from within the same class, from other classes, or even from other assemblies (if the method is accessible).

csharp Copy

```
int result = AddNumbers(5, 3); // result will be 8
```

Method Overloading:
Method overloading is a feature in C# that allows you to define multiple methods with the same name but different parameter lists (number, types, or order of parameters). The compiler determines which method to call based on the arguments provided during the method call.

Here's an example of method overloading:

csharp Copy

```
public int AddNumbers(int a, int b)

{
```

```
    return a + b;
}

public int AddNumbers(int a, int b, int c)
{
    return a + b + c;
}

public double AddNumbers(double a,
double b)
{
    return a + b;
}
```

In this example, there are three methods named AddNumbers, but they differ in their parameter lists. The compiler will choose the appropriate method based on the number and types of arguments passed during the method call.

Method overloading is particularly useful when you want to provide multiple ways to perform a similar operation, making your code more flexible and easier to use.

Method Signatures:
The method signature consists of the method name and the parameter list (number, types, and order of parameters). Method overloading is based on method signatures, not on the return type. In other words, you cannot overload methods based solely on different return types; the parameter lists must differ.

Methods are essential for modularizing code, promoting code reuse, and improving code organization and readability. By understanding how to define, call, and overload methods, you can write more efficient and maintainable code in C#.

Arrays and Collections

Arrays and collections are fundamental data structures in C# that allow you to store and manipulate groups of related items. In this lesson, we'll explore arrays and various collection types in C#.

Arrays:

An array is a collection of elements of the same data type stored in contiguous memory locations. Arrays have a fixed size, which is determined when they are created.

Declaring and Initializing Arrays:

csharp

Copy

```
// Declaring an array of integers int[]

numbers;


// Initializing an array with values numbers

= new int[] { 1, 2, 3, 4, 5 };
```

// Declaring and initializing in one step int[]

scores = { 85, 92, 77, 68, 94 };

// Creating an array with a specified size
int[] grades = new int[5]; // All elements are initialized to 0

Accessing Array Elements:
Array elements are accessed using an index, which starts from 0:

csharp Copy

scores[0] = 90; // Assigning a value to the first element

int firstScore = scores[0]; // Accessing the first element

Arrays in C# can have multiple dimensions (e.g., two-dimensional arrays for representing matrices or grids).

Collections:

While arrays have a fixed size, collections in C# are resizable and provide more flexibility and functionality for working with groups of items. The System.Collections namespace in C# provides several types of collections, including:

1. **List<T>**: A generic list that can dynamically grow and shrink as needed. It provides methods for adding, inserting, removing, and searching elements.

   csharp

   Copy

   ```
   List<string> names = new List<string>();
   names.Add("Alice");
   names.Add("Bob"); names.Insert(1,
   "Charlie");
   ```

2. **Dictionary<TKey, TValue>**: A collection of key-value pairs, where each key is unique. Dictionaries are useful for associating values with unique keys for efficient lookup.

csharp

Copy

```
Dictionary<int, string> students = new
Dictionary<int, string>(); students[1]
= "Alice"; students[2] = "Bob"; string
name = students[1]; // "Alice"
```

3. **HashSet<T>**: An unordered collection of unique elements. HashSets are useful for quickly checking if an item exists in the collection.

csharp

Copy

```
HashSet<int> uniqueNumbers = new
HashSet<int>(); uniqueNumbers.Add(5);
uniqueNumbers.Add(10);
uniqueNumbers.Add(5); // Duplicate
ignored
```

4. **Queue<T>**: A first-in, first-out (FIFO) collection, where elements are added to the end and removed from the front. csharp

   Copy

   ```
   Queue<string> queue = new
   Queue<string>();

   queue.Enqueue("Alice");

   queue.Enqueue("Bob");

   string person = queue.Dequeue(); // "Alice"
   ```

5. **Stack<T>**: A last-in, first-out (LIFO) collection, where elements are added and removed from the same end (top). csharp

   Copy

   ```
   Stack<int> stack = new Stack<int>();

   stack.Push(1); stack.Push(2); int

   number = stack.Pop(); // 2
   ```

These collections provide various methods and properties for adding, removing, and manipulating elements, as well as iterating over the collection using loops or LINQ (Language Integrated Query).

Choosing the appropriate data structure (array or collection type) depends on your specific requirements, such as whether you need a fixed-size or resizable collection, the order in which elements are added or removed, and the operations you need to perform on the collection.

Chapter 3: Object-Oriented Programming Essentials

Object-Oriented Programming (OOP) is a programming paradigm that revolves around the concept of objects, which are instances of classes. In C#, OOP principles are deeply ingrained in the language, and understanding them is crucial for writing efficient, maintainable, and scalable code. In this lesson, we'll explore the essential concepts of OOP in C#.

Classes and Objects:
A class is a blueprint or template that defines the properties (data) and methods (behavior) that an object of that class will have. An object is an instance of a class, created from the class blueprint.

csharp

Copy

```
// Defining a class
class Person
{
   // Properties (data)
public string Name;
public int Age;

   // Method (behavior)
public void Greet()
   {
      Console.WriteLine($"Hello, my name is
{Name} and I'm {Age} years old.");
   }
}
```

// Creating an object (instance) of the Person class

Person person1 = new Person();

person1.Name = "Alice"; person1.Age = 25;

person1.Greet(); // Output: Hello, my name is Alice and I'm 25 years old.

Encapsulation:
Encapsulation is the principle of bundling data (properties) and methods (behavior) together within a class, and controlling access to the class members. This is achieved through access modifiers like public, private, protected, and internal.

csharp Copy class

BankAccount

{

  // Private field (data hiding)

private decimal balance;

```
    // Public property (encapsulation)
public decimal Balance
    {
        get { return balance; }
set
        {
            if (value >= 0)
balance = value;            else
                Console.WriteLine("Invalid balance
amount.");
        }
    }

    // Other members...
}
```

Inheritance:

Inheritance is the ability to create a new class (derived class) based on an existing class (base class). The derived class inherits all the properties and methods from the base class and can add new members or override existing ones.

csharp Copy

```
// Base class class

Animal

{

   public void Eat() {
Console.WriteLine("Eating..."); }

public void Sleep() {

Console.WriteLine("Sleeping..."); }

}


// Derived class class

Dog : Animal
```

```
{
   public void Bark() {
Console.WriteLine("Woof!"); }
}
```

```
// Creating an object of the derived class
Dog dog = new Dog(); dog.Eat(); //
Output: Eating... dog.Bark(); // Output:
Woof!
```

Polymorphism:
Polymorphism is the ability of an object to take on many forms. It allows objects of different classes to be treated as objects of a common superclass. This is achieved through method overriding (providing a new implementation of a method in a derived class) and method overloading (defining multiple methods with the same name but different signatures).

csharp Copy

```
class Animal

{

   public virtual void MakeSound()
{ Console.WriteLine("The animal makes a
sound."); }

}


class Dog : Animal

{

   public override void MakeSound()
{ Console.WriteLine("Woof!"); }

}


class Cat : Animal

{

   public override void MakeSound()
{ Console.WriteLine("Meow!"); }
```

```
}

// Polymorphic behavior
Animal animal1 = new Dog();
animal1.MakeSound(); // Output: Woof!

Animal animal2 = new Cat();
animal2.MakeSound(); // Output: Meow!
```

Abstraction:
Abstraction is the process of hiding complex implementation details and exposing only the essential features or behaviors to the user. In C#, this is achieved through abstract classes and interfaces.

csharp

Copy

```
// Abstract class abstract
class Shape
```

```
{
    public abstract double GetArea();
}

// Derived classes class
Rectangle : Shape
{
    public double Width { get; set; }
public double Height { get; set; }

    public override double GetArea() =>
Width * Height;
}

class Circle : Shape
{
    public double Radius { get; set; }
```

```
    public override double GetArea() =>
Math.PI * Radius * Radius;
}
```

By understanding and applying these OOP concepts, you can write modular, reusable, and maintainable code in C#. OOP principles facilitate code organization, code reuse, and the ability to model real-world entities and relationships within your programs.

Introduction to Object-Oriented Programming (OOP)

Object-Oriented Programming (OOP) is a programming paradigm that models realworld entities as objects, which have properties (data) and methods (behavior). OOP revolves around four main principles: encapsulation, inheritance, polymorphism, and abstraction. These principles help in writing modular, reusable, and maintainable code.

1. **Encapsulation**:
   Encapsulation is the practice of bundling data (properties) and methods (behavior) together within a class, and controlling access to the class members through access modifiers
   like public, private, protected, and internal. This helps in data hiding and provides a clear interface for interacting with the class.

2. **Inheritance**:
   Inheritance is the ability to create a new class (derived class) based on an existing class (base class). The derived class inherits all the properties and methods from the base class and can add new members or override existing ones. This promotes code reuse and

helps in creating hierarchical relationships between classes.

3. **Polymorphism**:
   Polymorphism is the ability of an object to take on many forms. It allows objects of different classes to be treated as objects of a common superclass. This is achieved through method overriding (providing a new implementation of a method in a derived class) and method overloading (defining multiple methods with the same name but different signatures).

4. **Abstraction**:
   Abstraction is the process of hiding complex implementation details and exposing only the essential features or behaviors to the user. In C#, this is achieved through abstract classes and interfaces. Abstract classes cannot be instantiated, but they can have

abstract methods (without implementation) and concrete methods (with implementation). Interfaces define a contract that classes must implement, specifying a set of methods and properties that the implementing classes must provide.

Here's a simple example to illustrate these concepts:

csharp

Copy

```
// Base class (encapsulation) class
Animal
{
   private string name;


   public string Name
   {
```

```
        get { return name; }
set { name = value; }
    }

    public void Eat()
    {
        Console.WriteLine("The animal is
eating.");
    }

    public virtual void MakeSound()
    {
        Console.WriteLine("The animal makes
a sound.");
    }
}
```

```
// Derived class (inheritance) class
Dog : Animal
{
   public void Bark()
   {
      Console.WriteLine("Woof!");
   }

   // Method overriding (polymorphism)
public override void MakeSound()
   {
      Console.WriteLine("Woof! Woof!");
   }
}

// Abstract class (abstraction) abstract
class Shape
```

```
{
    public abstract double GetArea();
}


// Interface (abstraction) interface
IDrawable
{
    void Draw();
}
```

In this example, the Animal class demonstrates encapsulation by bundling the name property and Eat method together. The Dog class inherits from Animal and overrides the MakeSound method, illustrating polymorphism. The Shape abstract class and IDrawable interface demonstrate abstraction by defining abstract members that must be implemented by derived classes or implementing classes, respectively.

OOP provides a structured approach to software development, making it easier to manage complexity, promote code reuse, and model real-world entities in software systems. By leveraging these principles, developers can create more maintainable, extensible, and scalable applications.

Classes and Objects

Classes and objects are fundamental concepts in Object-Oriented Programming (OOP). A class is a blueprint or template that defines the properties (data) and methods (behavior) that an object of that class will have, while an object is an instance of a class created from that blueprint.

Defining a Class:

In C#, you define a class using the class keyword, followed by the class name, and a pair of curly braces {} enclosing the class members (properties and methods). csharp Copy class Person

```
{
  // Properties (data)
public string Name; public
int Age;

  // Method (behavior)
public void Greet()
  {
    Console.WriteLine($"Hello, my name is
{Name} and I'm {Age} years old.");
  }
}
```

In this example, the Person class has two properties (Name and Age) and one method (Greet()).

Creating Objects:
To create an object (instance) of a class, you use the new keyword followed by the class name and parentheses ().

csharp

Copy

Person person1 = new Person();

After creating an object, you can access its properties and methods using the dot notation .. csharp Copy

person1.Name = "Alice"; person1.Age

= 25;

person1.Greet(); // Output: Hello, my name is Alice and I'm 25 years old.

Constructors:
Constructors are special methods in a class that are automatically called when an object is created. They are used to initialize the object's properties with desired values.

csharp

Copy class

Person

```
{
    public string Name;
    public int Age;

    // Constructor
    public Person(string name, int age)
    {
        Name = name;
        Age = age;
    }

    public void Greet()
    {
```

```
    Console.WriteLine($"Hello, my name is
{Name} and I'm {Age} years old.");
  }
}

// Creating an object and initializing
properties using the constructor Person
person1 = new Person("Alice", 25);
person1.Greet(); // Output: Hello, my name
is Alice and I'm 25 years old.
```

Encapsulation:

Encapsulation is the principle of bundling data (properties) and methods (behavior) together within a class, and controlling access to the class members through access modifiers like public, private, protected, and internal. This helps in data hiding and provides a clear interface for interacting with the class.

csharp Copy class

BankAccount

```
{
   // Private field (data hiding)
private decimal balance;

   // Public property (encapsulation)
   public decimal Balance
   {
      get { return balance; }
set
      {
         if (value >= 0)
balance = value;            else
            Console.WriteLine("Invalid balance
amount.");
      }
```

```
    }

    // Other members...
}
```

In this example, the balance field is marked as private, preventing direct access from outside the class. Instead, a public

property Balance is provided, which encapsulates the logic for setting and getting the balance value.

Classes and objects are fundamental building blocks of Object-Oriented Programming in C#. By creating classes and instantiating objects, you can model realworld entities, encapsulate data and behavior, and create reusable and maintainable code.

Properties and Methods

Properties:

Properties are members of a class that represent the data or characteristics of an object. They act as intermediaries between the private fields of a class and the external code, providing controlled access to those fields.

Here's an example of a simple property:

```
csharp

Copy class

Student

{

   private string name; // Private field


   // Property

public string Name

   {

      get { return name; }

set { name = value; }
```

```
    }
}
```

In this example, the Student class has a private field name and a public property Name. The get accessor returns the value of the name field, while the set accessor sets a new value for the name field.

Properties can also provide additional logic or validation when getting or setting their values. For example:

csharp Copy class

```
BankAccount
{
    private decimal balance;

    public decimal Balance
    {
```

```
        get { return balance; }
set
        {
            if (value >= 0)
balance = value;
            else
                Console.WriteLine("Invalid balance
amount.");
        }
    }
}
```

In this case, the set accessor of the Balance property ensures that the balance cannot be set to a negative value.

Methods:

Methods are functions or procedures that define the behavior or operations that an object can perform. They encapsulate the logic or functionality of an object. Here's an example of a simple method:

csharp Copy

```csharp
class Circle
{
    public double Radius { get; set; }

    public double CalculateArea()
    {
        return Math.PI * Radius * Radius;
    }
}
```

In this example, the Circle class has a property Radius and a method CalculateArea() that calculates the area of the circle based on its radius.

Methods can accept parameters and return values. They can also be overloaded, which means you can define multiple methods with the same name but different parameter lists (number, types, or order of parameters).

csharp Copy

```csharp
class Calculator
{
    public int Add(int a, int b)
    {
        return a + b;
    }

    public double Add(double a, double b)
    {
        return a + b;
    }
}
```

In this example, the Calculator class has two Add methods, one that takes two integers and another that takes two doubles.

Properties and methods work together to encapsulate the state (data) and behavior of an object. Properties provide controlled access to the object's data, while methods define the operations or actions that the object can perform.

By using properties and methods, you can achieve encapsulation, one of the key principles of Object-Oriented Programming (OOP). Encapsulation helps in data hiding, provides a clear interface for interacting with objects, and promotes code reusability and maintainability.

Constructors and Object Initialization

Constructors:

- Constructors have the same name as the class they belong to.
- A class can have multiple constructors, known as constructor overloading, which allows objects to be created with different sets of parameters.
- If no constructor is defined in a class, C# provides a default parameterless constructor automatically.

Here's an example of a class with a constructor:

csharp

Copy class

Person

```
{
   public string Name { get; set; }
public int Age { get; set; }


   // Constructor
```

```
    public Person(string name, int age)
    {
        Name = name;
        Age = age;
    }
}
```

In this example, the Person class has a constructor that takes two parameters (name and age) and initializes the Name and Age properties of the object being created.

You can create objects using the constructor like this:

csharp

Copy

```
Person person1 = new Person("Alice", 25);
Console.WriteLine($"Name:
```

{person1.Name}, Age: {person1.Age}"); // Output: Name: Alice, Age: 25 **Constructor Overloading**:

As mentioned earlier, a class can have multiple constructors with different parameter lists, known as constructor overloading. This allows you to create objects with different sets of initial values.

csharp

Copy class

Person {

```
    public string Name { get; set; }
public int Age { get; set; }    public
string Address { get; set; }


    // Parameterless constructor
public Person() { }
```

```
// Constructor with parameters for Name
and Age
    public Person(string name, int age)
    {
        Name = name;
        Age = age;
    }

    // Constructor with parameters for
Name,
Age, and Address
    public Person(string name, int age, string
address)
    {
        Name = name;
        Age = age;
        Address = address;
    }
```

}

In this example, the Person class has three constructors: a parameterless constructor, a constructor with parameters for Name and Age, and a constructor with parameters for Name, Age, and Address.

You can create objects using the appropriate constructor based on the available data:

csharp Copy

Person

person1 =

new

Person(); //

Using the

parameterl

ess

constructor

Person person2 = new Person("Bob", 30); // Using the constructor with Name and Age

Person person3 = new Person("Charlie", 40, "123 Main St."); // Using the constructor with Name, Age, and Address **Object Initialization**:

C# also provides a shorthand syntax for object initialization, called object initializers. This syntax allows you to initialize object properties at the time of object creation without using a constructor.

csharp

Copy class

Person

{

public string Name { get; set; }

public int Age { get; set; }

}

```
// Object initialization
Person person1 = new Person { Name =
"Alice", Age = 25 };
```

In this example, the person1 object is created, and its Name and Age properties are initialized using the object initializer syntax.

Constructors and object initialization are essential for properly setting up objects with the desired initial state. Constructors provide a structured way to initialize object properties, while object initializers offer a concise syntax for simple initialization scenarios.

Inheritance and Polymorphism

Inheritance:

Inheritance is the ability to create a new class (derived class) based on an existing class (base class). The derived class inherits all the properties and methods from the base class and can add new members or override existing ones.

Here's an example:

csharp Copy

```
// Base class class
Animal
{
   public string Name { get; set; }

   public void Eat()
   {
      Console.WriteLine("The animal is
eating.");
   }

   public virtual void MakeSound()
   {
```

```
        Console.WriteLine("The animal makes
a sound.");
    }
}

// Derived class class
Dog : Animal
{
    public void Bark()
    {
        Console.WriteLine("Woof!");
    }

     // Method overriding       public
override void MakeSound()    {
        Console.WriteLine("Woof! Woof!");
    }
```

}

In this example, the Dog class is derived from the Animal class. It inherits the Name property and the Eat() and MakeSound() methods from the base class. Additionally, it has its own Bark() method and overrides the MakeSound() method with a new implementation specific to dogs.

Polymorphism:
Polymorphism is the ability of an object to take on many forms. It allows objects of different classes to be treated as objects of a common superclass. This is achieved through method overriding (providing a new implementation of a method in a derived class) and method overloading (defining multiple methods with the same name but different signatures).

csharp Copy

```
// Base class class
Animal
{
   public virtual void MakeSound()
   {
      Console.WriteLine("The animal makes
a sound.");
   }
}

// Derived classes class
Dog : Animal
{
   public override void MakeSound()
   {
      Console.WriteLine("Woof! Woof!");
   }
```

```
}

class Cat : Animal
{
    public override void MakeSound()
    {
        Console.WriteLine("Meow!");
    }
}

// Polymorphic behavior Animal
animal1 = new Dog();
animal1.MakeSound(); // Output:
Woof! Woof!

Animal animal2 = new Cat();
animal2.MakeSound(); // Output: Meow!
```

In this example, the Dog and Cat classes inherit from the Animal class and override the MakeSound() method with their specific implementations. The polymorphic behavior is demonstrated when animal1 and animal2 objects, which
are instances of the derived classes Dog and Cat, are treated as instances of the base class Animal. The appropriate MakeSound() method implementation is executed based on the actual object type at runtime.

Inheritance and polymorphism work together to promote code reuse, extensibility, and flexibility in OOP. Inheritance allows you to create new classes based on existing ones, inheriting their properties and methods, while polymorphism enables objects of different classes to be treated as objects of a common superclass, leading to more generalized and flexible code.

These principles are crucial in building maintainable, scalable, and modular software systems, as they allow you to model real-world relationships between entities and write code that can be easily extended and modified without disrupting existing functionality.

Interfaces and Abstract Classes

Interfaces:

An interface is a contract that defines a set of properties, methods, and events that a class must implement. It specifies what the class should do, but not how it should do it. In other words, an interface defines the behavior or capabilities that a class should have, without providing any implementation details.

Here's an example of an interface:

csharp Copy

```
interface IShape
```

```
{
   double CalculateArea();
double CalculatePerimeter();
}
```

Any class that implements the IShape interface must provide implementations for the CalculateArea() and CalculatePerimeter() methods. csharp Copy

```
class Circle : IShape
{
   public double Radius { get; set; }

   public double CalculateArea()
   {
      return Math.PI * Radius * Radius;
   }
```

```
    public double CalculatePerimeter()
    {
        return 2 * Math.PI * Radius;
    }
}
```

Interfaces promote abstraction, code reuse, and flexibility. Multiple classes can implement the same interface, allowing for polymorphic behavior and interchangeability of objects based on the interface contract.

Abstract Classes:

An abstract class is a special type of class that cannot be instantiated (you cannot create objects of an abstract class). Instead, it serves as a base class for other classes to inherit from. Abstract classes can have both abstract members (methods or properties without implementation) and non-abstract members (with implementation). Here's an example of an abstract class:

csharp Copy

```
abstract class Shape
{
    public abstract double CalculateArea();

    public void DisplayInfo()
    {
        Console.WriteLine("This is a shape.");
    }
}
```

In this example, the Shape class is an abstract class with an abstract method CalculateArea() and a non-abstract method DisplayInfo(). Any class that inherits from the Shape class must provide an implementation for the CalculateArea() method.

csharp Copy

```
class Circle : Shape
{
    public double Radius { get; set; }

    public override double CalculateArea()
    {
        return Math.PI * Radius * Radius;
    }
}
```

Abstract classes provide a way to define a common base for related classes and enforce a certain structure or behavior. They can also have non-abstract members that provide default implementations that derived classes can inherit or override.

Key Differences:

- An interface cannot have any implementation, while an abstract class can have both abstract and nonabstract members.

- A class can implement multiple interfaces, but it can inherit from only one base class (although that base class can inherit from another base class, forming an inheritance hierarchy).
- Interfaces define a contract for classes to implement, while abstract classes provide a common base for related classes and can also define default implementations.

Milton Keynes UK
Ingram Content Group UK Ltd.
UKHW021350201024
2278UKWH00020B/51

9 781806 251254